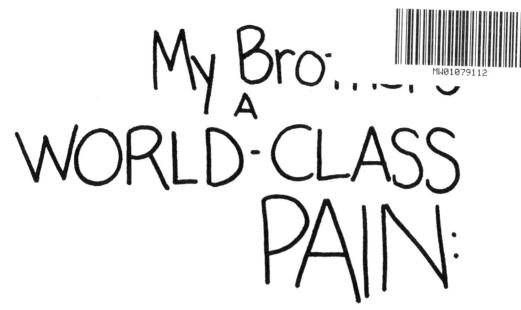

My Brother's A WORLD-CLASS PAIN:

A Sibling's Guide to ADHD/Hyperactivity

Michael Gordon, Ph.D.
Professor, Department of Psychiatry
Director, ADHD Program
Upstate Medical University at Syracuse

Illustrations and design
Janet H. Junco

GSI Publications, Inc.
P.O. Box 746, DeWitt, New York 13214
1-800-550-ADHD
Ph: (315) 446-4849 Fax: (315) 446-2012
E-Mail: info@gsi-add.com
www.gsi-add.com

GSI
PUBLICATIONS, INC.

Special thanks to Drs. Russell A. Barkley, Harvey C. Parker, Ruth C. Burton, and Wendy E. Gordon, for reviewing yet another manuscript. They are kind and patient friends. I also am very much indebted to my junior staff: Kristen Whitlock, Jennifer Gillman, Alexander Gordon, and Joshua Gordon. -M.G.

4th Printing, October 2007

ISBN 10: 0-9627701-2-4
ISBN 13: 978-0-9627701-2-8

GSI Publications, Inc.
P.O. Box 746, DeWitt, New York 13214
1-800-550-ADHD
Ph: (315) 446-4849 Fax: (315) 446-2012
E-Mail: info@gsi-add.com
www.gsi-add.com

GSI
PUBLICATIONS,INC.

To my younger brother, David,
who tought me more than he might ever know

FOREWORD

The story that you're about to read shines light on the oft-forgotten group of those affected by Attention Deficit Hyperactivity Disorder (ADHD), namely the brothers and sisters of ADHD children. While they frequently bear the brunt of the ADHD child's impulsiveness and distractibility, siblings usually are not afforded opportunities to understand the nature of the problem and to have their own feelings and thoughts addressed.

Children who read this story will be introduced to many of the basic concepts involved in understanding ADHD. More importantly, they will gain an appreciation of the demands that having a sibling with special needs places on all family members. Siblings will likely see many of their own frustrations and resentments voiced by Timmy's sister.

This book conveys a spirit of energetic problem solving which is so critical to a family's adjustment. It also sends the clear message to siblings of the ADHD child that they can play an important role in bringing about change. While not everyone will be able to manage the stoicism displayed by Timmy's sister, many youngsters might be more able to contribute to the process of coming to terms with this disorder. After all, every ounce of family support can bring pounds of relief.

Sandra Freed Thomas, R.N.
Former President, Children with Attention Deficit Disorders (CH.A.D.D.)
National Support Group

My brother's a pain. Not an ordinary pain like a lot of little brothers and sisters can be. I mean a world-class, non-stop, mind-numbing, make-you-want-to-hurt-somebody pain in the neck.

The kid just doesn't know how to quit doing *anything*. You should try watching TV with him. We sit on the couch together to watch a program. Within seconds his feet start banging and he's bouncing on the cushions. I get seasick watching TV in our own living room! But I can deal with that. What drives me nuts is when he starts making humming noises. He gets so loud that I can barely hear the program.

Off he goes for a drink. Back he comes with a toy. Out comes a question about the show. Off he goes for another drink. Back he comes with an airplane model he wants to put together. Out come ten more questions.

I'm saving all my birthday money so I can buy my own TV to keep in my room.

He drives my parents totally insane. You should see him at the dinner table. You may not be sure that the sun will rise tomorrow, but you can count on Tim knocking a glass of something over at dinner tonight. He doesn't seem to do it on purpose. He just never thinks about what he's doing or where he's going. I told Dad that we should put a sewer drain under Tim's chair so that all the food and milk he spills have a place to go.

He didn't seem so bad when Mom brought him home from the hospital. Actually, he was a cute baby who smiled a lot and had these funny little dimples when he laughed. He was fun to take care of and I'd play peek-a-boo with him for what seemed like hours. (Sometimes my friends would come over and we'd take turns seeing how many times we could get him to burp after he had his bottle.)

But then he got to be two years old and that was the end of the cute stuff. That kid could get into more trouble than I ever thought humanly possible.

He might have been sitting there harmlessly

for a minute, but I could turn my head for two seconds and he'd be off faster than a race car. Under the couch, on the counters, into the garbage can, out the door, over the gate...he was always your basic accident waiting to happen.

It made me nervous when my mother asked me to watch him because I was always afraid he'd hurt himself and I'd get into trouble for not being responsible. I once asked my Mom if I could chain him to the oak table in our family room. She didn't think that would be such a great idea. I wasn't sure if she was more worried about Timmy or the oak table.

5

One Sunday morning we all woke up and Mom went in to get Timmy up for church. No Timmy. I don't think she started losing control at that point, but she got real edgy when none of us could find him upstairs. Or downstairs. Or in the basement. Or in the yard.

He outdid himself that morning. Dad found him half way down the street with his favorite toy penguin tucked under his arm. As best we could tell, he was going to visit a lady who has this pretty flower garden. That was the day we put special locks real high up on the doors.

Then there was the time that Timmy thought it would be neat to pretend he was an airplane by jumping off of our roof. Timmy moves around a lot, but even he can't fly. He fell right onto the patio furniture and broke his arm. We're always going to the emergency room because Timmy does so many dangerous things. The nurse there said that they should have a private room ready for us 24 hours a day.

The problem for me was that he never could keep himself busy. All my friends' little brothers and sisters would play with toys, color pictures, or do other quiet activities. Not Timmy. You couldn't keep him busy for longer than a minute. And you couldn't sit him down to teach him anything. He lost interest in a flash. It was frustrating.

I don't want to sound mean, but being with Timmy in public can be extremely embarrassing. He's a master at saying the wrong thing, and he gets terribly wound up when other people come over or when we go to another family's house for dinner. He gets noisy and zooms all over. It's as if he gets overexcited by what's going on and he can't slow himself down.

I was so upset on my birthday. I got
my parents to let me have a bunch of
friends over for a pajama party, and I
spent all kinds of time putting up
decorations and trying to make it special. Unfortunately,
we spent most of the evening trying to get Tim away from
us. He was being such a pest. He got so bad that my Dad
took him out to a movie so we could have our party in
peace. My friend, Jody, shook her head and said, "How do
you ever stand it?"

I have to admit that having a brother like Timmy does have its advantages. For one thing, my parents are so busy worrying about him that I can get away with murder. I get into a lot less trouble than most of my friends because my parents think I'm almost perfect compared to Timmy. Look, I'm no angel but next to Timmy I'm pretty close to it. They must figure I'm the world's most responsible daughter because they have what must be the world's most impossible son. Maybe that's why they give me so much freedom.

While Tim drives us crazy at home, he's even worse at school. He races through all his work and has an awful time paying attention. He'll blurt out answers before he's even heard the whole question and he clowns around too much. My mom is in the principal's office so often dealing with Timmy's school problems that one of my friends actually thought that she worked there.

You won't believe this: Tim's teacher called last night (she talks with my parents all the time). She said that working with Tim over the past six months has convinced her that it is time to retire from teaching and move to Florida. She mentioned something about not having the energy she once had. We think she was kidding, but I'd probably feel the same way if I had to get Tim to sit and do work every day.

I feel badly for Tim, though. He usually thinks that he's doing just fine and then acts absolutely shocked when he fails a subject. He doesn't seem to connect how he's behaving with what will happen to him. It's a shame because he wants to do well and to please the teacher.

I do have to say that things got much better when my parents brought Tim to a doctor (he's called a psychologist) so that they could find out why he moves around so much and has problems paying attention. This doctor asked my parents a lot of questions and gave Timmy these special tests to see how smart he was and to figure out if he had more trouble than most kids learning and paying attention.

When all the tests and talking were finished, the doctor told my parents that Timmy has a problem called "Attention Deficit Hyperactivity Disorder" or ADHD. It's what they call what happens when somebody has problems paying attention even when they really try. My parents said that kids with ADHD do poorly in school because their brains don't let them slow down and pay attention just to the important things that are happening around them.

I actually heard about ADHD before because I have a cousin named Jerry who's older than Timmy but acted just like him when he was the same age. My aunt and uncle had him tested and found out that he was Hyperactive (which is what they used to call ADHD years ago). Believe it or not, Jerry was even worse than Timmy. And my dad said that Jerry's father, my Uncle George, had more trouble paying attention and sitting still than any person who ever lived. My dad said that Grandpa used to tie Uncle George to a tree just to keep him out of the way for a while.

We found that ADHD often shows up more in some families than in others. My mom says that having ADHD can run in families, like having red hair or being real good at math or having blue eyes.

Knowing Timmy has a real problem has helped. I don't get quite so mad at him and think that he's just a brat. And I understand a little better when my parents have to deal with him in special ways. But how nice can I be when I find my favorite books scribbled on or my radio in a million pieces (he likes taking things apart)? My dad told me it was okay to get angry with Tim as long as I don't rip him limb from limb. (I wouldn't anyhow, but I've thought about it because he can get me so angry.)

I was a little worried at first that my parents would use the ADHD to make excuses for everything wrong that Timmy did. I didn't want them to be going around telling me I should just ignore Timmy's bad behavior because he had this problem.

I can tell you that it hasn't worked out that way at all. My mom says that knowing Timmy has ADHD helps everyone to understand why he gets into trouble. But, if anything, they're much more strict with him now than they used to be.

Dad says that Timmy's got problems that are hard to fix overnight and that we all have to work at finding ways to help him keep it together. That was hard for me to accept because I wanted him to get rid of his ADHD absolutely IMMEDIATELY. It was plain hard to be patient and get excited about little changes when I was really wishing for big differences in how he behaved. I remember being frustrated when my parents would seem overjoyed just because Timmy had a temper tantrum "only" three days of the week instead of five. I would think to myself, "Big deal! This is such great progress?" Then Mom said that we had to keep a good attitude and that meant making the most of small steps in the right direction. She said that we needed to trust that eventually all the small steps would add up to a large leap forward.

For quite a long time we went as a family to see the psychologist. At first I didn't like the idea at all because I thought it would be embarrassing and we'd have to talk about private things. I also wasn't very comfortable at first answering all of his questions. And besides, I wasn't the problem by a long shot.

It turned out that the sessions with the psychologist were helpful because he explained all about ADHD and helped me understand why Timmy had so many problems at school and at home. But the most important part of our going to the psychologist was that he got us to work out ways of cutting down on all the yelling that would happen so often in our house. A lot of our talking had to do with setting up very clear rules, rewards, and punishments for Tim so he could start to learn that he needs to think about what he does before he goes ahead and gets into trouble. The bad part was that they also made more rules for me.

Rules are showing up everywhere in our house now. There are rules on the refrigerator, taped to Timmy's wall, and listed in the playroom. We have rules about listening the first time when we're told to do something, rules about not getting mouthy, rules about not fighting, rules about our behavior at the table and in public. I told my mom the other day that pretty soon we'll need one of those fancy supercomputers to keep track of all the rules.

To be honest, though, our house runs a lot more smoothly with everybody knowing what's expected and what happens if we break a rule. I've also noticed that my parents are much calmer when they punish us now because we've already discussed what the punishment would be for breaking the various rules. Before we had fixed punishments, I think they would punish us worse because they'd be angry at that moment and come up with something unfair. I also like knowing ahead of time what the consequences are because you never have to wonder what's going to happen.

The other important part of going to the psychologist was that it got all of us thinking about ways to solve the problems that keep coming up with Timmy. Rather than just getting frustrated or angry, we're trying to work on the problems with Timmy's behavior and schoolwork by acting like scientists trying to find a solution to some tricky puzzle.

To give you an example: Timmy always has had trouble going right to sleep because he'd fool around a lot. Yelling at him wouldn't help at all. Then my parents made a deal

with him. If Timmy went right to bed without any trouble, he could have a cinnamon roll for breakfast the next morning. Don't ask me why, but Timmy will do just about anything for a cinnamon roll. As a matter of fact, eating cinnamon rolls is about the only thing Timmy will sit to do quietly. He loves them so much that he'll really work at going to bed on time so that he will get his prized cinnamon roll. Ever since they worked this out, Timmy actually is more likely to get right to bed. Notice I said "more likely". There aren't tasty enough rolls in the world to settle Tim down when he's super wound up.

I think I had a good idea. Timmy's almost impossible when he has to do homework. It's not a pretty sight to say the least. I call it "Five seconds of work, ten minutes of messing around." I told my parents that Timmy does better if somebody's in the room with him when it's time to do homework. You don't have to sit right with him, just be nearby and remind him to keep working. So I started to do my homework at the other end of the kitchen table where he works. I also promised him that I'd play a minute of basketball for every minute he pays attention to his homework. It works pretty well most of the time and I actually get my own homework done better.

When we first made up all of these games with special prizes, I didn't think it was right because I figured it was like bribing him to be good. And bribing people is bad,

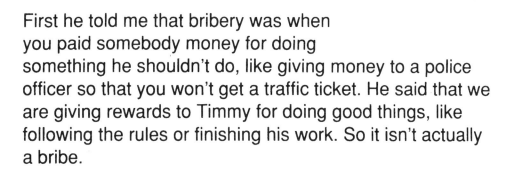

isn't it? So I eventually got the nerve to bring it up at one of the sessions with our psychologist. It took a little courage because I worried he'd think I was being fresh. Believe it or not, he thanked me for asking such a good question!

First he told me that bribery was when you paid somebody money for doing something he shouldn't do, like giving money to a police officer so that you won't get a traffic ticket. He said that we are giving rewards to Timmy for doing good things, like following the rules or finishing his work. So it isn't actually a bribe.

He also said that we need to really make it worth Timmy's while to follow the rules because it is so hard for him. It will be easier for Timmy to follow rules if we make it very important to him.

I had an idea of what the psychologist was talking about because I HATED doing the dishes and would do anything to get off having to clean up the table after dinner, even though it was one of my chores. At first my parents would just punish me when I "forgot" to do the dishes. That would make me mad. But then they changed  and said I could earn an extra quarter every night if I went ahead and did the dishes without a fuss. I still HATE to do the dishes but I like the extra money so it is worth getting them done without a hassle. (In case you're wondering, they don't pay me for every job I do. They said that most of my chores I needed to do because everyone in the family has to help out. They just come up with something special if it's a real hard chore or if I do an extra good job.)

Anyhow, I eventually figured that we aren't really bribing Timmy to be good. We are just making things more interesting and worthwhile for him so he'll be more likely to pay attention and finish what he's started.

One of the hard things about being Timmy's sister is that he gobbles up all of my parents' time. Mom and Dad spend so much time trying to find ways of getting him to pay attention that they pay almost no attention to me. They're always off to schools or doctors or counselors. Things got even worse when my parents became involved in this group where a whole lot of parents work together to help kids like Timmy. I think it's neat that they're working so hard to help others, but I can't tell you the last time we had a relaxed weekend. And my mother's on the phone even more than I am!

Sometimes I've gotten very angry about how much time they spend with Tim. I know that he has special problems and all, but I get upset when I feel left out. When I was younger I thought that I should start misbehaving and doing poorly in school so my parents would worry about me a little more. I decided against that plan when I thought about what my friends would think if I suddenly started acting weird.

I don't want to forget to tell you about the medicine Timmy started taking. You might think it's strange (I certainly did), but they have medicines that help kids pay attention better. My parents didn't start Timmy on the medicine right away because they wanted to learn all about it first. They also wanted to see if there were other things that could help enough so he wouldn't need medicine. But eventually they decided it was worth trying.

I was worried at first that they might be drugging him in ways that would make him strange and different. I also thought that he may become addicted like they talk about with people who abuse drugs. I found out from the psychologist, though, that it wouldn't make Timmy act like somebody different. He also said that Timmy wouldn't become addicted to the medicine.

I have to say that it really seems to help. Timmy's calmer and he actually seems to think more before he runs off and gets into trouble. And it hasn't changed his personality at all. He's still Timmy. He just isn't as squirmy and all over the place.

When he's taking the medicine it's much easier to play a board game with him and he's not so likely to go flying off. I know it was a hard decision for my parents, but I think it does help Timmy. The only problem I can see is that he eats less at lunch time and gets hungry later on. He's lucky because he gets to eat later when the medication has worn off.

One other thing I have to tell you about the medicine: When I saw how much better he behaved while he was on it, I wanted him to take it ALL the time (which he can't do because he wouldn't fall asleep at night). If he was being difficult when he wasn't on the medicine or if it was wearing off, I'd scream to my

Mom, "Timmy really needs his medicine now. He's impossible." Or if I got extremely angry at him I'd say something like, "You must need more of that medicine 'cause you're acting like a complete jerk!"

My parents got on me fast for that kind of talk. They told me that they didn't want Timmy to get the idea that the medicine controlled his behavior and decided whether or not he'd be good. They're trying to get him to feel responsible for what he does whether or not he's on the medicine. I guess I can see their point. I wouldn't want Timmy thinking that he could blame all of his problems on not having enough medicine, or that he couldn't be good unless he was taking his pill.

I can't tell you that all of the rules and time with the doctor and medicine has turned my bother into a gentle puppy, but he's no longer quite such a wild dog! It definitely has helped us deal with him better and he doesn't get into nearly as much trouble.

It's funny, ever since he's been better behaved, I've been getting scolded much more often. The psychologist said that I was getting into more trouble now because Timmy's better behavior gives me room to misbehave. He said I no longer had to play the role of the suffering sister (psychologists talk like that). That may be, but I just think my parents have more time and energy to keep an eye on me. I can't get away with nearly as much nowadays.

Sometimes I wonder what will happen with Timmy. He is still cute and I admit that he's about the friendliest kid you ever met. We call him "The Ambassador" because he introduces himself to anybody and everybody no matter where we are. We can't take two steps in the shopping mall without somebody shouting "Hi" to him. Everybody knows Timmy.

And you never have to guess what's on his mind. Whatever comes into his head comes right out of his mouth without anything stopping it. You should have been there at the grocery store last week. This really overweight lady was in front of us in line and one of the things she was buying was a gallon of chocolate ice cream. Tim walked right up to her and, not wanting to be mean or anything, told her that she really shouldn't buy the ice cream because it makes you fat and she was already too fat and it wouldn't be healthy for her to get even fatter. The part I couldn't believe was that the lady thanked him, told him he was right, and asked him to put the ice cream back in the freezer. Only Timmy could get away with that!

It's funny how everybody thinks he's absolutely adorable and nice even when he causes so much trouble. I think it's because people have this sense that he's not getting into trouble 'cause he's mean or rotten, but because it's hard for him to stop himself. And he has this way of saying something nice or smiling charmingly just when you're about to kill him. Dad says that Timmy's smile has been the main thing that's kept the kid alive for the past seven years.

If you have a brother with ADHD like Timmy, let me tell you that it sort of changes your life and isn't always very easy to deal with. Kids like Timmy can get you incredibly mad. And you can also get angry at your parents for spending so much time with them.

I guess in some ways, though, it sort of teaches you that not everybody's perfect and that families sometimes have to learn to work out problems together. I know that I talk with my Mom and Dad a lot more than my friends talk with their parents, and I think it's because we've spent so much time discussing Timmy and learning how to solve problems together. And it's kind of a challenge to see if you can figure out clever ways of trying to get him to pay attention and behave himself. I told my aunt the other day that I might want to be a teacher when I get older and work with kids who have special problems.

And let me tell you, life's never boring around here. Especially when Timmy has a friend over or gets mischievous. As a matter of fact, I hear some funny noises coming from the basement and I'll bet you anything that Timmy's at it again. I think I'll go check it out and see what he's into now!